FEB 1 7

W9-AWE-707

Behind the Wheel of a
DRAGSTER

BY ALEX MONNIG

The Child's World®
childsworld.com

Published by The Child's World®
1980 Lookout Drive • Mankato, MN 56003-1705
800-599-READ • www.childsworld.com

Acknowledgments
The Child's World®: Mary Berendes, Publishing Director
Red Line Editorial: Design, editorial direction, and production
Photographs ©: Cal Sport Media/AP Images, cover, 1; Manfred Steinbach/
Shutterstock Images, 4; iStockphoto, 7; Jne Valokuvaus/Shutterstock Images,
8; R.C. Young/iStockphoto, 12; David Allio/Icon SMI/Corbis, 15; Michael
Stokes/Shutterstock Images, 16; Tony Kurdzuk/Star Ledger/Corbis, 18; Action
Sports Photography/Shutterstock Images, 20

ISBN 9781634074292

LCCN 2015946272

Printed in the United States of America
Mankato, MN
December, 2015
PA02282

Table of CONTENTS

Chapter 1

GREEN MEANS GO

Your fingers are tightening around the steering wheel of your dragster. Your heart is pounding so hard you feel like it is going to burst through your chest. It is the final **heat** of one of the biggest drag races in the world.

You have raced perfectly all day. You won six heats against six different drivers. That sort of performance is what it takes to reach the final of a major drag racing competition. Being successful when going head-to-head with the best drivers in the world requires incredible technique and timing. The stress can make you nervous.

The races usually last less than five seconds. But a lot can go wrong in that tiny amount of time. Any single mistake can cost you the race. All the hard work, training, and previous heat victories could be for nothing if your timing is off by even one-tenth of a second.

◄ **Dragster crews work on the vehicle between each race to make sure it is in top form.**

But you have trained for years for this. You have spent hundreds of hours working on your car. You race in the top classification. That means your vehicle is long and thin, almost coming to a point at the front. Each dragster is built specifically for its driver. Yours is black with blue and white lightning bolts on the side.

You know what to do. You know when to do it. But that does not make it any easier. The pressure is starting to get to you. What if your timing is slightly off when the starting light turns green? What if you shift incorrectly and lose speed? That split-second slowdown could be the difference between winning and losing.

Your mind is going through all the things that could go wrong. But it should be focused only on the race. In a moment, the starting lights will glow. No more time for worrying. It is time to race.

Drivers in each lane have a series of lights that lets them ▶ know when to start the race.

Chapter 2

DRAGSTER DETAILS

Your cousin was a huge drag racing fan. You looked up to him when you were young. You thought he was cool. So that meant you became a huge drag racing fan, too.

The two of you dreamed of owning a dragster together. You both saved money over many years. You practiced in cars owned by other racers around town. Finally, you got into the game yourselves. You and your cousin bought a car together.

Some of your friends also loved drag racing. They became your pit team. Your cousin started as the team's main driver. But you ended up being better at racing. You still remember the day he said you should be the team's main driver.

That was almost ten years ago. Your cousin and friends still make up your team. But after rising up through the ranks of racing, your car is much different.

◄ **There are many different types of dragsters. Some look more like everyday cars.**

Your current car is a top-fuel dragster, the fastest classification of dragster. Top-fuel dragsters look unique. A typical top-fuel dragster is about 25 feet (7.6 m) long. It weighs about 2,320 pounds (1,052 kg). And it has larger wheels in the back than in the front. These help with control during extreme acceleration.

Slight differences in car weight can give you the edge you need to win. Your team members constantly tinker with your dragster. They help keep the car's weight balanced and steering tuned. They know how to get the most out of the car, and you, because you have worked together for so long.

Most standard cars have engines that sit in the front of the vehicle. Dragsters used to be like this, too. But things changed in the 1970s. Driver Don Garlits built a dragster with the engine behind the driver. Now, all top-fuel dragsters are built this way.

A large wing sits behind you when you drive. The wing connects to the top of your car. It also creates downward air pressure. This force helps keep you and the dragster from rising off the ground when you get up to extreme speeds.

During your races, you travel only 1,000 feet (305 m). The short distance means dragsters have to get up to speed quickly. That is your favorite part.

Riding in a dragster feels like being launched by a rocket. The cars can get up to 100 miles per hour (161 km/h) in less than one second. And they can reach 300 miles per hour (483 km/h) in less than four seconds. At top speed, top-fuel dragsters reach more than 330 miles per hour (531 km/h).

DON GARLITS

Don "Big Daddy" Garlits is one of the most revolutionary drivers in drag racing history. His **transmission** blew up during a 1970 race. It split his car in half. His right foot was cut off. So Garlits went to work. He invented a car with the engine behind the driver. This helped keep the driver safer in case of an accident. In the next two years, all top-fuel dragster drivers switched to Garlits's model.

Chapter 3

FINE TUNING

You and your cousin quickly learned there is more to drag racing than speed. Knowing how to finish a race safely is even more important. When your car travels at top speeds, it creates a lot of friction. That friction creates extreme heat. Just the slightest mishap can spell disaster for both you and your car.

Your cousin's dad, your uncle, took you to your first race. That day there was a horrible crash. One of the cars went up into the air suddenly. Car parts flew everywhere. The dragster even caught on fire.

You could not believe it when the driver walked away from the wreck. Your uncle told you it was because of safety rules designed to keep drivers safe during disasters.

All drivers wear protective gear when behind the wheel. You remember zipping up your jumpsuit for your first race. It felt like

◀ Top-fuel dragsters have wide tires that grip the racetrack.

a heavy-duty pair of winter pajamas. The jumpsuits are heat and fire resistant. They also help keep you cool during races.

You wore gloves that helped you grip the wheel. And you had boots and a helmet with a visor. These things combine to keep you as safe as possible in extreme racing conditions.

The National Hot Rod Association (NHRA) has safety rules all drivers must follow. Every car has to have a fire extinguisher in it. You must also have a specific type of harness. It keeps you in your seat. The harness has a quick-release function. This way you can quickly get out of the vehicle, if necessary.

Speeding at more than 300 miles per hour (483 km/h) makes slowing down dangerous. Your uncle taught you that braking too quickly could make you crash. You could spin out of control and flip over. This is why drivers use parachutes. It is another NHRA rule. Parachutes help cars safely slow down after racing.

Drivers and maintenance teams are like tailors. And their cars are like high-priced tuxedos. You and your team fit your car especially for you. Dragsters cannot be too light. They need to be able to withstand the rigors of racing. But they also cannot be too heavy. They need to be able to go as fast as possible. Finding the perfect weight for your dragster has taken years. It was only

Dragster drivers wear harnesses, helmets, and protective ▶ suits to keep them safe during races.

▲ Top-fuel dragsters burn hundreds of
dollars of fuel during each race.

when you and your team mastered this skill that you started
winning races.

Your car has become an extension of you. It is almost like
another limb. You need to be in complete control of it at all times.
Any sudden movement can cost you a race.

Perfecting performance took years of practice. That practice
started before you even got in your car. Lightning-quick reflexes
and timing are keys to winning. Somebody might be the best
driver in the world. But that does not matter if he or she messes
up the start.

So you spent dozens of hours on reflex training. You tried several different programs for timing practice. You got used to reacting as soon as the green light glowed.

But training in the driver's seat is the most important. You did thousands of practice runs once you became the team's main driver. You learned how the weight of the car shifted when you performed certain actions. You got a feel for shifting gears. Shifting is one of the most important parts of racing. Keeping the transition smooth when gaining speed takes precision.

Each time down the track can cost thousands of dollars due to fuel costs. Luckily you do not have to pay for everything anymore. A large car producer now sponsors your driving team. It pays for car parts and race entries. All you have to focus on is winning.

CHANGING THE RACE

Official drag races used to run for 1,320 feet (402 m). That changed in 2008. That year, driver Scott Kalitta died. He raced in a dragster class called funny car. His engine exploded during a race. So the NHRA shortened races to 1,000 feet (305 m). This change gave racers less time to build speed. It also gave them more time to slow down after the finish line.

Chapter 4

RACE DAY

You have continued to hone your craft. You and your team practice daily. Small changes are continually made to your car. All of that has made you one of the top drivers in the world. Now you are in the final heat of a big event. The driver who crosses the 1,000-foot (305-m) mark first will win the entire competition.

You roll up to the starting line. Before getting all the way there, you do a burnout. To do this, you push down on the gas pedal with the brakes on. This makes your back tires spin. Smoke comes out. It looks like the tires are burning. Burnouts warm up and clean the tires. This makes them better suited for racing.

Next comes staging. You pull up the car to the starting line. Each inch of the drag race is important. Racers pull up to a precise spot. There is a red-laser light near the ground that runs across the starting line. When a tire blocks that laser, the car is ready to race.

◄ **Drag racers burn out before races to prepare their tires for the race.**

▲ **Parachutes help dragsters slow down at the end of races.**

Now you are focused on the "Christmas tree." That is a name for the starting lights. It is not an actual Christmas tree. Instead, it looks like two stoplights connected side by side. There are lights at the top that glow when staging is complete. Then there are two columns of five large round bulbs below. First are three amber lights. Below them is a green light. At the bottom is a red light. The lights flash one by one. When the green light flashes it is time to go. The red light turns on only for a foul start. A foul start is when a racer starts to accelerate too soon.

The timing between flashes is always the same. This allows you to practice. You have gotten the timing down to the exact moment when the green light glows.

You are nervous. But instinct is taking over. The first amber light glows, and your muscles tense up. The second amber light is on. Now the third. Your reflexes are perfect as the green light glows. You glide through the gears as your car gains speed.

About 4.4 seconds later, you cross the finish line. You won. Everything happened so fast. You do not even remember your feelings before the green light. All the practice has guided your thoughts and actions. You are a professional drag racer. And now you are a champion.

GLOSSARY

acceleration (ak-sel-uh-REY-shuhn): Acceleration is the increase of speed. Your dragster gains speed during acceleration.

classification (klas-uh-fi-KAY-shuhn): A classification is a category that consists of similar things. Top-fuel dragsters are the highest classification of dragsters.

friction (FRIK-shuhn): Friction occurs when two materials rub together. The friction between your tires and the road at high speeds causes high temperatures.

harness (HARH-niss): A harness is a collection of straps that keeps something from moving too much. Drivers rely on a harness to keep them safely in their seats while racing.

heat (heet): A heat is round of races. In drag racing, each heat is between two drivers.

shift (shift): In racing, to shift is to change from one gear to another. You shift gears to gain speed when accelerating.

transmission (trans-MISH-uhn): The transmission sends power from a car's engine. The transmission in Don Garlits's car malfunctioned and caused his engine to explode.

TO LEARN MORE

Books

Georgiou, Tyrone. *Top Fuel Dragsters*. New York: Gareth Stevens Publishing, 2011.

Kelley, K. C. *Drag Racing*. Tarrytown, NY: Marshall Cavendish Benchmark, 2010.

Miller, Dean. *Becoming a Pro Auto Racer*. New York: Gareth Stevens Publishing, 2015.

Web Sites

Visit our Web site for links about dragsters:
childsworld.com/links

Note to Parents, Teachers, and Librarians: We routinely verify our Web links to make sure they are safe and active sites. So encourage your readers to check them out!

SELECTED BIBLIOGRAPHY

"History Detectives: Drag Racing." *PBS.org*. Oregon Public Broadcasting, n.d. Web. 25 Jun. 2015.

Levy, Art. "Icon: Don 'Big Daddy' Garlits." *Florida Trend*. Trend Magazines Inc., 3 Oct. 2012. Web. 25 Jun. 2015.

"NHRA Drag Racing 411." *NHRA.com*. NHRA, n.d. Web. 25 Jun. 2015.

Webster, Larry. "Anatomy of a Top-Fuel Dragster." *Popular Mechanics*. Hearst Communications, 24 Jan. 2011. Web. 25 Jun. 2015.

INDEX

ABOUT THE AUTHOR

Alex Monnig is a freelance journalist from Saint Louis,
Missouri, who now lives in Sydney, Australia. He graduated
with his master's degree from the University of Missouri in
2010. During his career, he has spent time covering sporting
events around the world.